A QUESTION AND ANSWER STORYBOOK

Why is soap so slippery?

and other

bathtime questions

by Catherine Ripley

illustrated by Scot Ritchie

OWL BOOKS

Why is Soap So Slippery? and other bathtime questions

Owl Books are published by Greey de Pencier Books Inc.,
179 John Street, Suite 500, Toronto, Ontario M5T 3G5

OWL, *Chickadee* and the Owl colophon are trademarks of Owl Communications.
Greey de Pencier Books Inc. is a licensed user of trademarks of Owl Communications.

Distributed in the United States by Firefly Books (U.S.) Inc.,
230 Fifth Avenue, Suite 1607, New York, NY 10001

This book was published with the generous support of the Canada Council,
the Ontario Arts Council, and the Government of Ontario through the Ontario Publishing Centre.

Special thanks to Dr. Randall Brooks, National Museum of Science and Technology;
Johnson & Johnson; The Ontario Arts Council; Gordon and Marion Penrose;
Susan Woodward, Royal Ontario Museum; the teachers and children whom I visited in the
winter of 1993 at Manotick Public School (Jill Cutler, Judy Wood and their classes)
and at St. Leonard's Elementary Separate School (Nancy Beddoe, Milly Donaldson,
Dianne Landriault and their classes) for inspiration; Sheba, Kat and Trudee for their
careful, friendly editing; Mary for making the words and pictures work together;
Scot for his inviting, fabulous illustrations; and my family for their patience and support.

DEDICATION

For Bruce, the cleanest person I know.

Canadian Cataloguing in Publication Data

Ripley, Catherine, 1957–
Why is soap so slippery? and other bathtime
questions

ISBN 1-895688-34-5 (bound). – ISBN 1-895688-39-6 (pbk)

1. Science – Juvenile literature. I. Ritchie,
Scot. II. Title

Q163.R5 1995   j500   C94-932491-4

Design and Art Direction: Mary Opper

Also available:
Do the Doors Open by Magic? and other supermarket questions

Printed in Hong Kong

A   B   C   D   E   F

Contents

How can hot and cold water run out of the same tap?

Surprise . . inside the wall behind the faucet there are two pipes! One pipe brings hot water from your hot water tank. The other pipe brings cold water directly from your neighborhood water supply. When you turn the tap, you let hot or cold water run into the faucet. Turn the tap a little and a trickle of water flows through, turn the tap a lot and the water gushes out! If you let cold and hot water into the faucet at the same time, the water from the two pipes mixes together so that warm water runs out.

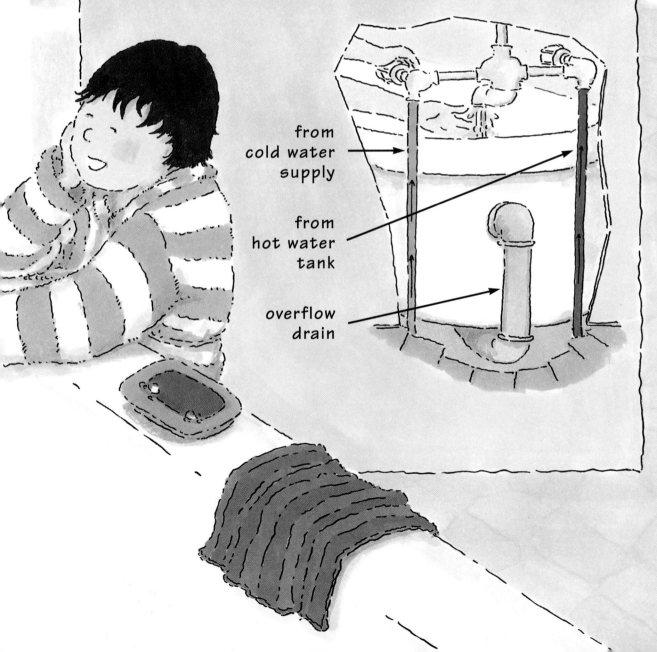

from cold water supply

from hot water tank

overflow drain

Why do I have to brush my teeth?

Inside your mouth are tiny, tiny living things called bacteria. When you don't brush, food sticks to your teeth, and the bacteria eat the sugars in it. As they do, they let out waste that's full of acid strong enough to melt the hard outer coating of your teeth. Then, uh oh, the acid makes holes! These holes are called cavities. By brushing your teeth, you get rid of the sugars that the bacteria like to eat. If the bacteria have nothing to eat, then there's no acid to make cavities in your teeth. That's why you brush.

To get rid of the leftovers. As you chew and swallow, your teeth and stomach turn, say, an apple into a soupy mush. The apple mush travels through your body becoming thinner and thinner. Some of it flows out of your small intestine into your blood and all around to feed the different body parts.

But there are always some leftovers! The leftover food mush in your large intestine becomes solid waste. Your kidneys take watery leftovers out of your blood, and send the liquid waste to your bladder. To get rid of all these leftovers, you go to the bathroom.

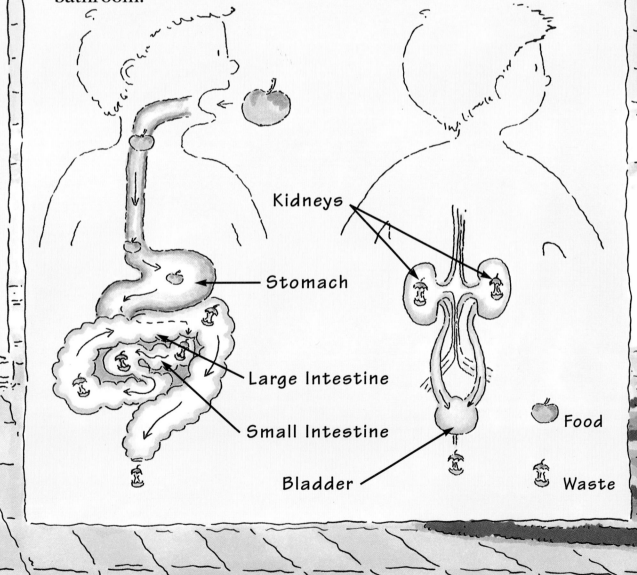

Kidneys

Stomach

Large Intestine

Small Intestine

Bladder

Food

Waste

Where does it go when I flush?

Down and out! Whoosh—the toilet water travels down a pipe from the toilet, through a pipe inside your home, and then out to a bigger pipe. If you live in the city, the water flows into an even bigger pipe under the street. Then it flows through bigger and bigger pipes on to a water treatment plant, where the toilet water is cleaned.

In the country, the pipe outside your house might carry the water into an underground septic tank, which is like a water treatment plant in your own backyard.

Water treatment plant

Pipes from houses

Animals don't have bathtubs ~ so how do they stay clean?

All sorts of ways. Believe it or not, zebras roll around in dirt to get clean! It's old skin and bugs they need to clean off. Chimps have a friend pick out the bugs and dirt from their fur, while cats use their tongues to lick themselves clean. Rhinos depend on the help of a special bird — the bird gets to have a meal of the pesky bugs it finds on the rhino's hide. And elephants shower or bathe in dust, or in water — without the soap!

Why is soap

All the better to clean you! Like all things, soap is made up of millions of molecules — tiny pieces so small you can't see them without a microscope. When soap gets wet, water molecules free up the soap molecules so that they can slip and slide around. They slip easily onto your skin, join with the dirt, and slide the dirt right off your body, leaving you clean as a whistle.

Because they are not like the tears in your eyes. When shampoo gets in your eyes, your eyes feel the difference right away. They send a "stinging" message to your brain: *Ow! Help! Something strange is here!* To get rid of the strange stuff, the brain tells your eyes to make more tears and wash the shampoo away. Some shampoos are specially made to be as much like the water in your eyes as possible. These "tearless" shampoos fool your eyes and don't sting.

Because they get too naked! Your skin is covered by a thin, thin coat of oil. When you are in the bath for a long time, the coat of oil is washed away. The bath water can then seep under your naked skin, making it swell up and wrinkle. On palms of your hands and the soles of your feet, the skin is thicker, so there's more skin to make big wrinkles.

Why does the floor feel colder than the bathmat?

Because of the heat leaving your feet. The hard, smooth tile floor feels colder because it carries the heat away from your feet. The more the heat flows out of your feet, the colder they feel. The soft, fuzzy bathmat feels warmer because the spaces between the fuzz hold the heat, and don't pull it away from your feet as quickly as the tile floor does. And so, the bathmat feels warm and the floor feels cold.

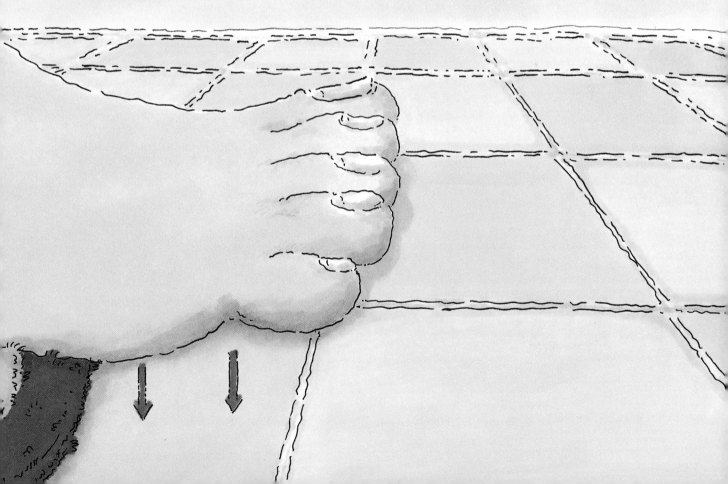

Why can I draw on the mirror?

Because the air is full of water. You usually can't see the water in the warm, wet air from your bath or shower. That's because the water is in its invisible form, called water vapor. But when water vapor lands on something colder than itself, like a mirror, it turns back into tiny drops of water. The drops make a thin layer, covering the mirror and making it white like a piece of paper. When you draw with your finger, it breaks the film apart to show the mirror underneath. Ta da — a picture!

Why is there a funny noise when the water drains away?

Because the drainpipe is like an upside-down drinking straw. As you suck on a straw, you make an empty space, called a vacuum, inside it. When you get to the bottom of the glass, there isn't enough juice left to fill the space.

Air rushes up the straw to help fill the space up. The juice and air slosh together and make a lot of noise. That's just what the last drops of water and air do when they rush down the drainpipe.

How do towels get dry by morning?

Because a drying towel is like a slo-o-o-o-o-w-ly boiling kettle. If you boil water in a kettle long enough, all the water will disappear. That's because the water turns into water vapor and leaves the kettle dry and empty. In the same way, if you leave a wet towel in a dry spot long enough, the water in the towel will slowly change into water vapor. Little by little, the invisible water vapor floats into the air and away from the towel, until it is dry.

Bath Bits

Ducks do more than just get clean when they preen, or run their feathers through their beaks. Their beaks carry oil from a gland at the back of their bodies and spread a thin coat of it all over, waterproofing their feathers.

Can you imagine disguising a bathtub as a tall set of dresser drawers? That's what some people did long ago to hide the bathtub in the bedroom. Why? Because there were no bathrooms yet!

When you blow a soap bubble, you fill a thin soap-and-water skin with enough air to make it float away.

Stop! Before you fill that glass to rinse your teeth, think about the fact that a dinosaur may have drunk that very same water millions of years ago. The water on Earth is used over and over and over and over . . . .